Dreamscapes And Imagination

Edited By Lynsey Evans

First published in Great Britain in 2024 by:

Young Writers
Remus House
Coltsfoot Drive
Peterborough
PE2 9BF
Telephone: 01733 890066
Website: www.youngwriters.co.uk

All Rights Reserved
Book Design by Ashley Janson
© Copyright Contributors 2024
Softback ISBN 978-1-83565-456-9
Printed and bound in the UK by BookPrintingUK
Website: www.bookprintinguk.com
YB0591G

FOREWORD

Welcome Reader, to a world of dreams.

For Young Writers' latest competition, we asked our writers to dig deep into their imagination and create a poem that paints a picture of what they dream of, whether it's a make-believe world full of wonder or their aspirations for the future.

The result is this collection of fantastic poetic verse that covers a whole host of different topics. Let your mind fly away with the fairies to explore the sweet joy of candy lands, join in with a game of fantasy football, or you may even catch a glimpse of a unicorn or another mythical creature. Beware though, because even dreamland has dark corners, so you may turn a page and walk into a nightmare!

Whereas the majority of our writers chose to stick to a free verse style, others gave themselves the challenge of other techniques such as acrostics and rhyming couplets.

Each piece in this collection shows the writers' dedication and imagination – we truly believe that seeing their work in print gives them a well-deserved boost of pride, and inspires them to keep writing, so we hope to see more of their work in the future!

CONTENTS

Edinburgh Steiner School, Edinburgh

Rosa Greenholm (10)	1
Laila Hollington (10)	2
Martha Jebsen Moore (10)	3
Leopold Szyszczakiewicz (9)	4
Isabella Emonts-Holley (9)	5
Athena Markson-Brown (10)	6
Niamh James (9)	7
Finbar Mackenzie (10)	8
Emma Miller	9
Annika Clegg (9)	10
Gabriel Chelvaiyah (10)	11
Corrie Mitchell (10)	12
Rosalie Boskamp (9)	13
Jaël Schwerzmann (10)	14
Veronika Mitchell (10)	15
Luna Herdlein (9)	16

English Martyrs' RC Primary School, Preston

Safaa Patel (8)	17
Helena Galka (9)	18

Hartford Manor Primary School and Nursery, Hartford

Hayley Aurora Yarwood (8)	19
Trinity Wilson (8)	20
Alice Duggan (9)	22
Herbie York (10)	24
Evie Woodward (10)	25
Hazel Harford (10)	26
Jasmine Lambert (9)	28

Benjamin Harper (7)	29
Annie Argent-Belcher (9)	30
JJ Waring (10)	31
Pearl O'Brien (9)	32
Emily Cawley (9)	33
Annabel Tickell (9)	34
Gabriella Brake (11)	35
Alexia Dickinson (7)	36
Emily Duggan (9)	37
Lillian Waite (9)	38
William Slaven (10)	39
Grace Smith (11)	40
Pahandi Heeralu Mohottalalage (7)	41
Ayla Danby (8) & Alice Davies (8)	42
William Tait (6)	43
Livvy Thompson (7)	44
Josie Marsland (8)	45
George Page (11)	46
Keira Gauterin (10)	47
Pippa Ellis (9)	48
Ava Patterson (9)	49
Lily Hickson (7)	50
Carson Lightfoot (9)	51
Amy Fazackerley (11) & Georgia Kindon (10)	52
Sam Gauterin (8)	53
Ivy Hendrix Godwin (6)	54
Olivia Humphries (8)	55
Paislee Barton (7)	56
Quinn Wray (7)	57
Rachel Parkhill (8)	58
May Hepworth (6)	59
Natalie Davies (8)	60
Maisie McAdam (6)	61
Harry Perris (11)	62
Noah Ochota (7)	63

Aeryka Stephens (7)	64
Evan Hepworth (9)	65
Arthur Goldspink (8)	66
Florence Bradburne (10)	67
Daisy Hinchliffe (7)	68
Evelina Ochota (10)	69
Alexander Kettle (8)	70
William Johnstone (10)	71
Dottie Briscall (7)	72
Eleanor Kettle (6)	73

Oakwood Primary School, Easter House

Abel Jackson (8)	74
Katerina Spanellis (8)	75
Ailidh Low (8)	76
George McQuade (8)	77
Edie-Beau Bunton (8)	78
Lewis McNally (9)	79

Pennthorpe School, Rudgwick

Rebecca Foster (10)	80
Maisie Watkins (10)	82
James Pinder (10)	83
Lara Hinchey (11)	84
William Pinder (10)	85
Oliver Bristow (11)	86
Olivia Church (11)	87
Aurelie Perkes (11)	88
Zara Watson (11)	89
Summer Faulding (10)	90
Anaya Thakkar (10)	91
Arthur Mitchell	92
AJ Morton	93
Callum Cambell-Yaxley (10)	94

St Alban's Catholic Primary School, West Molesey

Isabel Starkie Refoios Camejo (9)	95
Olivia Shitta (11)	96
Aleksy Stevens (9)	98

St Mary's Catholic Primary School, Madeley

David Aneke (12)	100
Cerys Thomas (10)	102
Annabeth Irvine (10)	103

St Paul's CE Junior School, Wokingham

Jonas Rothwell (8)	104
Anvi Mishra (10)	106
Akshara Uppuluri (8)	108
Gene Coleman (8)	110
Ethan Ang (11)	112
Zoe Tomlinson (10)	114
Laura Hicklin (10)	115
Kathryn McDonough (10)	116
Aanya Sandeep (9)	117
Georgia Stuart (10)	118
Joel Robertson (10)	119
Katerina Hopkins (10)	120
Elissa Feist Guerrero (9)	121
Millie Simms (10)	122
Freya Moore (10)	123
Evelyn Clements (10)	124
Oliver Radcliffe (9)	125
Darcie Withers (8)	126
Lauren Glover (9)	127
Ellie Wong (9)	128
Rosie Harrison (9)	129
Elvis Poon (9)	130
Anna Griffin (9)	131
Jayvis Chan (9)	132
Ahmad Alsayd (10)	133
Giorgia Alessandrini (9)	134
Adrianna Lau (8)	135
Gautam Singh (11)	136
Arya Partthepan (8)	137
Jiya Shah (7)	138
Isabella Guo (10)	139
Jacob Sheppard (9)	140
David Purle (11)	141
Leilah Abdelrahim (8)	142

Dhruvi G Patel (9)	143
Isobel Reid (10)	144
Sofia Hunt (9)	145
Laiba Khalil (10)	146
Arin Sahoo (8)	147
Zoe Shaw (8)	148
Mabel Hodson (8)	149
Adelaide O'Mahoney (10)	150
Hayden Li (9)	151
Aarna Singh (11)	152
Shiona Chatterjee (11)	153
Noah Brocklehurst-Waite (9)	154
Iris Yan (9)	155
Mithat Kaur (10)	156
Skye Chow (7)	157
Maia Garwood (10)	158
Jaya-Belle Barkes (8)	159
Sujay Venkatesh (8)	160
Violet Perry (9)	161
Natanya Philip (10)	162
Nathaniel Watson (10)	163
Alfie Nicoll (10)	164
Holly Haskins (9)	165
Sin Yan Ying (10)	166
Dennis Eaglesham (9)	167
Oscar Campbell (9)	168
Nikòs Cheema (8)	169
Alice Dimmock (10)	170
Fraiser Warner (10)	171
Daisy Rao (10)	172
Arjun Ravi (10)	173
Charlie Peacock (8)	174
Muffin Tang (9)	175
Theo Dunmow (9)	176
Sadie Grinter (10)	177
Isaac Gosling Baker (9)	178
Bethan Kirkaldy (9)	179
Irhaa Gillani (8)	180
Anjana Senthil Kumar (10)	181
Fraser Rhodes (10)	182
Fatimah Asad (10)	183
Ameya Sunil (9)	184

THE POEMS

Unicorn Dream

U nheard of beasts, wild, ferocious, galloping over meadows,
N one other than the mighty horned beasts themselves.
I n a torrent of hoof beats, they pass me and my horse.
"C ontinue," neighs the leader; my horse wants to leave.
O n again, on and on, they fade, they lessen, they are gone.
R unning, screaming. No, wait! I am safe in bed.
N o, they are gone; my horse is gone. I am safe; I am warm at home.

Rosa Greenholm (10)
Edinburgh Steiner School, Edinburgh

Sweet Dreams

In the dream I had that night
I was by a lake, silver and white
There was frost on the trees and frost on the ground
There was nowhere with frost not to be found
In an instant, I dived into the lake
Not a splash did I make
Instead of the normal things, you would see
I looked around myself with glee
Candy canes and lollipops
Sugarcanes and fruity drops
I picked a chocolate fish from the deep
This is a memory I will keep.

Laila Hollington (10)
Edinburgh Steiner School, Edinburgh

Flying Unicorns

The dream I had that night
My sleep was full of light
Amazing beyond words
All galloping in herds
Unicorns!
Grooming them through the day
Riding them through the night
Feeding them bales of hay
Energy for their flight
We flew into the sky
And watched the moon go by
I woke up suddenly
No more horses left to see.

Martha Jebsen Moore (10)
Edinburgh Steiner School, Edinburgh

In A Different World

S imilar to my garden, a world very weird,
T rotting unicorns, fire-breathing dragons,
R avens with wings as long as me,
A nd when I go to this world,
N ow and then, bells ring.
G iants are running away,
E lder trees grow big and then I wake up. Hey!

Leopold Szyszczakiewicz (9)
Edinburgh Steiner School, Edinburgh

The Maze Dream

R ound and round the maze I go,
A mazing things pass me,
B ouncing, that's what the rabbit loved to do,
B efore my eyes I see a flash,
I 've disappeared from the maze,
T ossing and turning I land back in my bed.

Isabella Emonts-Holley (9)
Edinburgh Steiner School, Edinburgh

Once Upon A Dream

Every night my cat
Arrives to sleep with me
To dream with me about
Silent streams and fish in a dish
He's late to sleep
He won't be pleased
The door is shut
He pushes, jumps
And click goes the handle.

Athena Markson-Brown (10)
Edinburgh Steiner School, Edinburgh

Dream

D ream that I had rabbits and tigers.
R un! The tigers are surrounding.
E verything is coming. Oh no!
A ttack! They are coming. That was a bad idea.
M y life is about to end.

Niamh James (9)
Edinburgh Steiner School, Edinburgh

Once Upon A Dream

F lashing fearless and funny
L ions leaping lightly
Y apping and
I gnorant and insolent
N ow I wake up and I realise it was a
G reat dream.

Finbar Mackenzie (10)
Edinburgh Steiner School, Edinburgh

Moon Dream

The silver moon is shining bright
High up in the silver light
Looking down at all the land
I see a face in the moonlit sand.

Emma Miller
Edinburgh Steiner School, Edinburgh

Dream

D are to jump over the
R ock down to
E arth
A nd away to the
M ountains.

Annika Clegg (9)
Edinburgh Steiner School, Edinburgh

Wind

A haiku

The winds gracefully
Dance, sing everywhere and blow
Dreaming through the night.

Gabriel Chelvaiyah (10)
Edinburgh Steiner School, Edinburgh

Nightmare

A haiku

A nightmare waits, still
Then creepily stalking, slow
Into the room, hard.

Corrie Mitchell (10)
Edinburgh Steiner School, Edinburgh

The Nightmare

A haiku

The nightmare watching,
Waiting as still as a stone,
Till I fall asleep.

Rosalie Boskamp (9)
Edinburgh Steiner School, Edinburgh

Fall From Horse

A haiku

In my dream at night,
My horse ran away and I'm
Sitting on the sand.

Jaël Schwerzmann (10)
Edinburgh Steiner School, Edinburgh

My Spell Dream

A haiku

Spells are beautiful
Whispers that touch the black sky
I feel it in me.

Veronika Mitchell (10)
Edinburgh Steiner School, Edinburgh

My Dream

A haiku

For my birthday, I
Got a magical pig who's
Called Peggy Herdlein.

Luna Herdlein (9)
Edinburgh Steiner School, Edinburgh

My Fears In Dreams

M onsters under my bed at night,
Y es, I know they give me a fright.

F ailure of my exams and tests,
E very time my heart beats in my chest,
A lways curled up like a cat, it's best,
R aging road drivers are so daring,
S piders are always scaring!

I n my dreams,
N o staying still.

D on't you think dreams come to you, both loud and shrill,
R owdy dogs, barking at the till,
E nd of sleep will be soon,
A monster waking me up at noon,
M y dream is gone, see you soon,
S uddenly, I find myself snuggled tight in my bed!

Safaa Patel (8)
English Martyrs' RC Primary School, Preston

Unicorn Land

U nicorn land is such a magical place.
N ever cry in such a place.
I ce and fire unicorns.
C orn everywhere and unicorns.
O ne unicorn is pink; everyone is different.
R enting unicorns is illegal.
N ever cry in such a place.

L anding on unicorns is such fun.
A my is my favourite; she is pretty.
N ever cry in such a place.
D erek is the only black one.

Helena Galka (9)
English Martyrs' RC Primary School, Preston

Magical Powers

M ermaids splash around in the sea and enjoy eating cake and sleeping in shells!
A day off for everyone and no one is unkind, and I make them be kind with my magic powers!
G randude takes us to school, and all we do is have fun because of my powers!
I am not tired, Martha and Mila are coming for a playdate to meet the kittens, how fun.
C amouflage my body to help me hide in the game of hide-and-seek!
A sparkling star appears at the click of a finger!
L ie on the floor asleep, as white as snow, the kittens wake up and start to chat to us!

P ancakes appear for everyone and to make them come, you just stand there!
O n the click of two fingers, my piano appears and I play a beautiful tune!
W hales swim around my bedroom and I can ride them whenever I like!
E verybody listens to each other because my power makes them quiet. Other people are speaking!
R ed roses and lovely lilies appear when I touch anything
S weet sound of birds singing (it has to be five seconds or over) to help you fall asleep!

Hayley Aurora Yarwood (8)
Hartford Manor Primary School and Nursery, Hartford

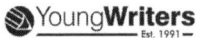

Just Like You

Once upon a starry night,
I had a dream of a light so bright,
And in that light was a little grey man,
Who smiled at me and took my hand.

His eyes were big and dark as night,
And at first, I was filled with fright.
But soon I could see, he meant me no harm
For those big, dark eyes were happy and warm.

He spoke to me with words never said,
For his mouth never moved but his words were in my head.
He asked if I would like to go for a drive
In his shiny spaceship that was parked outside.

On board were corridors of cosmic gleam,
And inside each room I saw curious things.
There were nick-nacks and trinkets and objects galore,
From pianos to footballs to bicycles and more.

We ran around, playing for the longest of whiles,
Until he exclaimed, "Gosh, look at the time,
I best get you back to bed before morning,
Or you'll spend the whole day stretching and yawning!

You may have been wondering why I came to visit?
I mean, when you think about it, it's not obvious! Is it?
For the longest time, I've had a quest to pursue.
My quest was to meet a friend just like you."

Trinity Wilson (8)
Hartford Manor Primary School and Nursery, Hartford

The Land Of My Imagination

I once had a dream,
It was so supreme.
It made me want to gasp and shout,
Gasp and shout and scream.

First, there was a dragon,
That swooped far and high
Then, there was a monster
That made me want to cry.

They brought me to a city where there were familiar faces,
It might not have been pretty,
But there were some human traces.

Then, a train flew along, made of cardboard boxes,
I don't know why, as I looked up to the sky,
The smell was smelly and toxic.

The trees were towering,
Tall and blue,
And it looked like they actually flew.

When I woke up,
And looked up at the ceiling,
I had a most peculiar feeling.

If this was all real,
As I believed,
Would I be sad,
Or would I be relieved?

Maybe it's all out there,
Far, far away,
Perhaps I'll see it again,
If I hope and pray.

Alice Duggan (9)
Hartford Manor Primary School and Nursery, Hartford

Natural History Museum

N othing much happens here
A lthough there may be hidden surprises
T he average day
U nique is one way to describe it
R eal historical things begin to stretch
A fter lock-up, they play
L eft to rampage all night long

H ating the sunlight
I t is because it bakes them
S izzles them up into ash
T o keep them out of mischief
O n the first flicker of sunlight, they return to statues
R eady for tomorrow
Y et nobody knows these secrets

M ost just see boring facts
U sually, there is silence for a minute or two after closing
S ecurity went home for tea
E verybody had gone but one
U nder the Statue of Liberty
M oments later they came to life...

Herbie York (10)
Hartford Manor Primary School and Nursery, Hartford

A Dragon's Flight

As the evening sun shone its light,
Me and Mirage were ready for flight.
His scales shimmered a silvery blue,
As we took off and away we flew.
I touched the clouds of the pretty pink sky,
I looked down at my town but I didn't want to cry.
The lights below glimmered a wonderful gold,
It was like the tales Mirage had told.
I watched the clouds darkening for a while,
It had felt as though we'd flown far more than a mile.
Mirage gave a grunt as if he had said,
"Now it's time for you to get to bed!"
I spluttered to say, "But what about you?"
"I'll always be there, in school too,
But no matter what, I'll be in your head."
And then I woke up and was in my bed.

Evie Woodward (10)
Hartford Manor Primary School and Nursery, Hartford

Asleep

Asleep in bed,
Almost dreaming,
I rest my head,
Grinning, beaming.
I dream of this,
I dream of that,
I dream of a giant bowler hat!

Asleep in bed,
Now I'm dreaming,
I feel the dread,
But can't hear screaming.
I dream of this,
I dream of that,
I dream of a terrifying tabby cat!

Asleep in bed,
Thought I was dreaming,
Decided to wed,
But what's the meaning?
I dream of this,
I dream of that,
I dream of a fairy that's very fat!

Asleep in bed,
No longer dreaming,
Need to get fed,
But Dad is cleaning?
I dream of this,
I dream of that,
Rolled out of bed and then went splat!

Hazel Harford (10)
Hartford Manor Primary School and Nursery, Hartford

Dreamland

Dreamland is a place where everyone goes,
What will you find there? Nobody knows.
You can eat with the lions,
And fly with the bats,
Dreams don't get much better than that.
In a dream that I once had,
I thought it was good and then it turned bad.
The sky turned black and started to smog,
Then the lake turned into a treacherous bog.
All of my worst fears started to form,
From out of the eye of the terrible storm.
Evil red eyes all turned to me,
It was a terrifying, scary sight to see.
Then a clown,
That was looking down,
Started to sing,
Then the evils went with a cute little ding.
Then a unicorn was my pet,
I won it in a lovely bet.

Jasmine Lambert (9)
Hartford Manor Primary School and Nursery, Hartford

The Land Of Sweets And Chocolate

One starry night I went to bed,
Delicious visions filled my head!
Chocolate rivers, chocolate seas,
Chocolate flowers and chocolate trees.
I walked around and saw some more,
A candy house with a toffee door!
Then I met a friend so nice,
Who offered me some sugar mice.
I looked at him and noticed that,
He wore a Maoam as a hat!
Then I saw to my surprise,
He had two sweets instead of eyes!
"Hello, my friend!" he said to me,
"Would you like to come and see,
A forest made of Haribo,
Where Tangfastics and Starmix grow?"
"Yes please, I really would!" I said,
But then I realised I was in bed.

Benjamin Harper (7)
Hartford Manor Primary School and Nursery, Hartford

Night Race

A dappled coat with a luscious, thick grey mane,
His nostrils flaring, ears alert, ready.
The wondrous creature tugged upon the rein,
With galloping hooves, powerful, steady.

And as the grand horse thundered down the track,
His strong hooves beat against the golden path.
Just then, my strong horse whinnied in triumph,
As the crowd roared and the rope tore in half!
The crowd exploded; I beamed in delight,
Those graceful legs had run and won the fight!

Then suddenly, I tossed, turned roundabout,
I thought I heard my mother give a shout.
I was staring at a blank bedroom wall,
Then I realised that no race won at all.

Annie Argent-Belcher (9)
Hartford Manor Primary School and Nursery, Hartford

Journey Through Enchanted Realms

In this land of fantasy, where dreams come to play,
You'll find yourself in an enchanting world every step of the way,
Through meadows of emerald and skies of sapphire-blue,
You'll find yourself in an enchanting world every step and view,
You'll explore a realm where the impossible will come true,
With my furry friend by my side, who is loyal and blue,
Together I discover wonders, both old and new,
Castle of shimmering gold, reaching for the stars,
Guarded by mythical creatures like dragons from afar,
In this fantasy land, where imagination takes flight,
You'll encounter fairies, wizards and magical light.

JJ Waring (10)
Hartford Manor Primary School and Nursery, Hartford

What I Once Dreamt About

Once I dreamt of a kingdom
Full of animals and mythical creatures
There were rainbows everywhere
And if one shone over you
You would know that you were brilliant

There was a beautiful queen
A handsome king
We would bow to them
And together we would sing
Because we were perfect together

In the academy
They decorated your rooms
With things you like and love
Like pictures of family
Maybe pet pictures too

The best thing was
You got to choose a pet
It could be a dog, a cat, a horse or even a dragon

That's what I dreamt about!

Pearl O'Brien (9)
Hartford Manor Primary School and Nursery, Hartford

The Royal Duck

In a world quite different to ours,
Past the distant plains of Mars.
It lies in wait in your head,
You can always find it in your bed,
This night, it took me to a plain,
I found a spider in bad pain,
It coughed and sneezed and danced about,
It was allergic to its web no doubt!
We hadn't walked for very long,
And we found a duck among a throng,
"The Royal Duck!" they cried in glee,
"Is it waiting just for me?"
It appeared, the duck had a name,
And as the country began to fade,
I waved goodbye to all my friends,
I hope to see the duck again.

Emily Cawley (9)
Hartford Manor Primary School and Nursery, Hartford

Once Upon A Fairy

Once upon a fairy,
When the breeze was nice and airy,
Tiptoeing on a toadstool,
Watching as the sun grew,
Swirling, swirling clouds on the horizon overhead,
Waiting and watching for the time to release their dread,
Running, fast and small,
Watching overhead,
Clouds of rain are forming over the blue sky,
Not able to touch the blazing heat of the sun,
Run quickly, run fast, or this could be the end,
Maybe you're a fairy with silver wings, and kindly,
So fly and fly 'til you're floating in space,
Scared of it all so you wake, nice and comfy in bed!

Annabel Tickell (9)
Hartford Manor Primary School and Nursery, Hartford

Dreams

When I was small,
I had a dream that one day I would be tall.

I would reach for the sky,
I would learn to fly,
And be the bravest of them all.

I could lasso the sun,
It would be great fun,
Living in Dreamland.

Now I am grown, I roam all on my own,
I've not reached the sky,
I've not learned to fly,
I'm not the bravest of them all.

I can't lasso the sun,
I miss when I was young,
When all was not as it seemed.

Though I could carry on,
And have great fun,
Dancing in my dreams.

Gabriella Brake (11)
Hartford Manor Primary School and Nursery, Hartford

The Magic Cave

M e and my auntie walk through a cave; we see fairies and crystals.
A shining waterfall glows in the spotlight as pixies appear.
G igantic flowers blossomed as we walked through the emerald grass.
I cicles sparkle and shine, and one day they will all be mine.
C rystals glow, as a moon in the night, and I dream about them.

C olourful gems glisten in the water, twinkling like stars.
A methyst appears like a dragon's eye.
V eins dangle down like raindrops falling.
E verything looks like a dream come true.

Alexia Dickinson (7)
Hartford Manor Primary School and Nursery, Hartford

In My Dreams

Close your eyes and dream,
Make sure you're safe and sound,
This will be extreme,
On a journey to your dreams.

Knights in gleaming armour,
Dragons flying high,
Witches cruel and evil charmers,
Monsters under beds.

Sky as dark as coal,
Tucked up in your bed,
Trapped inside a big, black hole,
Nearly witching hour.

Trapped inside a maze,
Feeling very lost,
Almost in a haze,
Wondering where to go.

This will happen,
This won't happen,
This might happen,
But only in my dreams.

Emily Duggan (9)
Hartford Manor Primary School and Nursery, Hartford

Lost In Nowhere

One day I find myself lost,
Lost in nowhere,
I see a flying bus zoom by,
Taking people to the moon;
There's also an ice cream van,
Playing a nice tune.
There are fairies dancing,
And twirling around;
There are aliens clanging,
And making a sound.
Everyone's looking,
Looking at me,
Whilst I simply wonder,
Where could I be?
There are dinosaurs roaring,
And beavers gnawing;
People shooting ice,
And trolls playing dice.
When suddenly I wake up with a big scream,
And find out that it was all a dream.

Lillian Waite (9)
Hartford Manor Primary School and Nursery, Hartford

My Dream For The Future

In the future, I hope all my dreams will come true
I hope to make videos, enjoyed by me and you
My dream isn't to get views, coming by the ton
I want my friends by my side, us all having fun
And when the day is done, I will rest my head
Having marvellous dreams, all whilst sleeping in my bed
I will dream of a land, quite similar to ours
Where inky monsters walk, I put enemies behind bars
I don't dream of being a superhero, all I need is my friends
Although this world wasn't my idea
I'm with it 'til the end.

William Slaven (10)
Hartford Manor Primary School and Nursery, Hartford

Fairy Tale

I wish I had a castle,
As big as can be.
I will have a dream,
In which I can touch the sky.
I will ride a pony to the moon,
Like a rocket ride to Cotton Candy Land.
I believe I could live to one thousand,
But I'm so young, at eleven.
The good ones go too soon,
Just like your sweet dreams.
Remember when we were young,
You believed you could touch the sky.
All those tales are over,
Now that you are old, you'll believe again.
One, two, three, touch the sky.

Grace Smith (11)
Hartford Manor Primary School and Nursery, Hartford

Magic Horses

The magic horses eat the scrumptious pie,
Who run all the way around the sky.

As they play with the boys,
And use their little toys.

And now they are sleeping,
While the diamonds are exploding.

When they wake up they hear,
A great big cheer.

And when they are walking,
They hear someone is talking.

Then they see a great big school,
Next to a deep, blue pool.

On their way to their house
They see a little mouse.

Pahandi Heeralu Mohottalalage (7)
Hartford Manor Primary School and Nursery, Hartford

My Dream

In my dream
I thought I was safe until I turned around,
Many scary faces turning round and round,
I ran and ran and ran,
I was full of terror
And then I found a place safe and sound where I could stay forever,
I love my land,
I love my life and I shall stay forever,
I will never leave this place, never, ever, ever
And if people think it's strange to dream that kind of thing,
Well, I don't care,
I'll shout everywhere,
That is my dream!

Ayla Danby (8) & Alice Davies (8)
Hartford Manor Primary School and Nursery, Hartford

It Was Saturday Night

It was Saturday night, I had the best dream,
About a magical blue football team.
They scored goals as easy as breathing air,
Long, curly, and wavy hair.
The boss was called Pep,
The striker was Álvarez
The midfielder was KDB,
The defender was me.
I wanted to be striker so I spoke to the boss,
Pep shook my hand. He doesn't like a loss.

I woke up the next day with my strip by my bed,
I soon realised it was just an incredible dream in my head.

William Tait (6)
Hartford Manor Primary School and Nursery, Hartford

Beach Dancing With Friends

I'm dancing at the beach,
I'm with my friends, Lilly, Darcie and Iris, they like to dance too.
I love to twirl, it makes me feel alive.
I can see the light blue ocean and I can feel the smooth, sparkly sand under my feet.
I can smell suncream and feel the warm breeze on my face.
I can taste the salt on my ruby-red lips, and I can hear the waves crashing like cymbals.
I can feel the sun's heat like blazing flames on my body.
I love being at the beach with my friends.

Livvy Thompson (7)
Hartford Manor Primary School and Nursery, Hartford

Unicorns And Fairies

In my dreams at night,
I see unicorns with bright pink wings,
Starlight tails, and starlight manes.
Flying and twirling,
They soar through the moonlight sky,
Waving their horns about.
In my dreams at night, I see magical fairies
With bright sparkly wings,
Helping animals when they're hurt,
Eating magical fruit,
Flying in the rainbows as well.

But every night, leave fruit,
But they disappear.
Maybe next year, they'll come back.

Josie Marsland (8)
Hartford Manor Primary School and Nursery, Hartford

My Dreams

I once had a dream
Where I was turned into cream
Another one, where I met Mr Edward Lear
With only one ear

I dream of more, as you will see
Of dragons, elves and fantasy
Of hobbit holes and monsters under the ocean blue
Whilst white and brown horses gallop through

To dream like me, you don't need to be smart
Or good at art
Or have lots of money
Or even to be well read
You just need imagination in your head.

George Page (11)
Hartford Manor Primary School and Nursery, Hartford

A Fairy-Tale Dream

Rainbow clouds fill the sky
I can fly so very high
I soar up high, I swoop down low
I go high up until I see a bungalow
Little pixies scattered around
In that house, I have found
A dancing cat named Mr Mic Tat
I fall asleep in this wondrous house
That's when I dream of a speaking mouse
What a wonderful house
I wake up smiling and beaming
That's when I realise that I am just dreaming.

Keira Gauterin (10)
Hartford Manor Primary School and Nursery, Hartford

Bunnies

B eautiful bunnies hop along the countryside
U nique, crunchy carrots get tasted with love,
N oisy gnawing from rabbit mouths spread across the universe,
N uts and acorns fall from the treetops, on top of the burrows,
I cicles, frost overnight being crushed away
E nds of carrots are being loved
S nowdrops fall on top of their tongues and get blown away.

Pippa Ellis (9)
Hartford Manor Primary School and Nursery, Hartford

In My Dreams

In my dreams, I can see
My life in front of me
A brilliant world for me to seek
Gifts and trinkets for me to keep
Inviting smiles for me to make
Never has life been any better
Every day I receive a letter
And it reads that I've got to go home
Until then when I'm in my little zone
I'll read and read
Of my dreams
Never forget to read and dream.

Ava Patterson (9)
Hartford Manor Primary School and Nursery, Hartford

Magic Days

Fairies pink as a peach,
They glow blue,
And sparkle prettily in the twinkling night sky.

Unicorns prancing around,
On the green, swashy grass,
Making dandelions float all around.

Princess's dimples are so sweet,
And they sing,
"Roses are red,
Violets are blue,
Sugar is sweet,
And so are you."

Lily Hickson (7)
Hartford Manor Primary School and Nursery, Hartford

Mermaid

M inutes after I wake up, I find myself in the sea.
E very day, after breakfast, I swim around my cave.
R ushing waves were heard for miles
M um shrieked, "Pirates invading!"
A ll of our gold and jewels were gone
I swam through the dark ocean waters
D iving up and down to claim back our gold.

Carson Lightfoot (9)
Hartford Manor Primary School and Nursery, Hartford

War

From the hundred-year war,
England and France,
To the World War,
Which had Hitler in a trance.
From peace and poppies,
Became our world.
They slept in heaven,
While we slept on Earth.
The world is still changing,
With wars by its side.
Earth is still in peace,
While heaven's on our mind.

Amy Fazackerley (11) & Georgia Kindon (10)
Hartford Manor Primary School and Nursery, Hartford

Strike A Goal

I kicked the ball and it went flying past the wall,
I hit it so hard and fast. I think it went over, the goalie wasn't that tall!
I wanted to score for my team, the best in all the land,
When I fall down, they help me up to stand.
The ball went straight into the net,
I was a hero, I was flying as high as a jet!

Sam Gauterin (8)
Hartford Manor Primary School and Nursery, Hartford

I Like This

What?
Oh, I'm sorry
Hi! My name is Ivy
So, let's get going!
Ivy went away
So my mum came
I got lost in London
Oh no!
But I saw my mum and dad, but Granny came too
I didn't like my granny
I got home
I really wanted to play about
So, what should we see in the next one?

Ivy Hendrix Godwin (6)
Hartford Manor Primary School and Nursery, Hartford

Daydream

D ays turn into night
A nd you close your eyes tight
Y our adventure has begun
D rift off and start your fun
R eflecting on the day gone by
E xcited and ready to fly
A mazing memories never forgotten
M istaking my bed and falling on my bottom.

Olivia Humphries (8)
Hartford Manor Primary School and Nursery, Hartford

Flying Magic

Flying magic in the sky
Delicate wings flutter by

In magical woodland together
They play, dancing, leaping
Jumping all day

Magic dust is sprinkled down
Like sheets of snow on the ground

Making children's dreams come true
Bringing happiness all year through.

Paislee Barton (7)
Hartford Manor Primary School and Nursery, Hartford

Famous

D esiring to be on stage, under the flashing lights.
R ubies and diamonds on my glamorous costume.
E merald-green stars scatter across the stage.
A udience claps and cheers, making me feel included.
M ighty loud music makes me start with butterflies and finish with a bow.

Quinn Wray (7)
Hartford Manor Primary School and Nursery, Hartford

What A Dream

I don't know how to explain,
I suddenly found a lane.
I wandered down to Memory Town,
Where the road ended with cobbles of brown.

A rainbow shot across the sky,
With colours so bright, it scorched my eye.
I caught my breath and stepped ahead,
And passing by a fairy sped.

Rachel Parkhill (8)
Hartford Manor Primary School and Nursery, Hartford

Your Special Night

In the night not a sight
Everybody asleep soundly, but
What's that noise?
It's the party, it's so fun
It's so fun.
At the party, where is the singer?
She looks just like the sun.
"I am nervous
I hope I do good."
That night, she was amazing.

May Hepworth (6)
Hartford Manor Primary School and Nursery, Hartford

Beautiful Butterfly

Butterfly, oh beautiful butterfly
I've seen you fly
You fly up high and down low
Your spots glimmer and gleam as you go
As everyone watches and admires you as you glide
Through the wind and show your moves
Oh butterfly, beautiful butterfly
Look how far you've come.

Natalie Davies (8)
Hartford Manor Primary School and Nursery, Hartford

School On Fire

I had a dream the school was on fire.
I could no longer hear the distant choir.
I felt scared.
How would all of this be repaired?
I saw people running,
But the fire engines were not coming.
I wanted this nightmare to end,
And to be safe again with my friends.

Maisie McAdam (6)
Hartford Manor Primary School and Nursery, Hartford

The 999 Emergency

On the 999 emergency, there were
Firemen, police and ambulance
All there ready to take action
Police roam the town and paramedics save lives
The firemen all muscly and strong
Save a cat from a tree
Now there are many more emergencies
Maybe you can help!

Harry Perris (11)
Hartford Manor Primary School and Nursery, Hartford

Sleep

S uper surprises, some are scary, some are happy
L ight turns on, what is it? A creepy clown!
E verything goes dark, I can't see a thing!
E xciting stories that never stop
P lenty of adventures and new discoveries.

Noah Ochota (7)
Hartford Manor Primary School and Nursery, Hartford

There's A Monster

I had a dream, it seems
There was a monster coming
It was running towards us, it wanted a friend
But we had to pretend because we were scared
Because we weren't prepared
It started crying
It was really trying to be a good monster.

Aeryka Stephens (7)
Hartford Manor Primary School and Nursery, Hartford

In The Harbour

In the harbour, in the dead of night
Not a soul was in sight
With captains lying down in bed
Dreaming of haddock and cod
The boats sitting still
The wintery water
With children watching the captains
Waiting for the morning.

Evan Hepworth (9)
Hartford Manor Primary School and Nursery, Hartford

Rugby

R ugby is a fine sport, it gives you bumps and bumps
U ps and downs, turns you round
G o rugby, it makes you hungry
B umps and lumps you get
Y ou get hurt and get back up again.

Arthur Goldspink (8)
Hartford Manor Primary School and Nursery, Hartford

Young

When I was young when I was small
When I wasn't tall at all
I would read and read for days on end
Until I got to the end of the book
After that my dreams were magical
My favourite books came alive.

Florence Bradburne (10)
Hartford Manor Primary School and Nursery, Hartford

All About Stitch

Stitch is an alien
He's cute, cool and crazy
He's the cuddliest of all
He loves Lilo
Angel loves Stitch
He's very cute
I love Stitch and you should love him too!

Daisy Hinchliffe (7)
Hartford Manor Primary School and Nursery, Hartford

Dreams

D elightful
R emarkable
E xciting
A mazing
M agical
S urprises

Maybe one day your dreams will come true.

Evelina Ochota (10)
Hartford Manor Primary School and Nursery, Hartford

Dream

D reams are wonderful,
R emember them all,
E xcept the scary ones,
A nd telling them to others,
M akes them come true.

Alexander Kettle (8)
Hartford Manor Primary School and Nursery, Hartford

Winter Islands

Snow glaciers,
Cold and frosty like a pool in winter,
The sun frozen over by clouds,
Angels soar in the sky,
Wishing to demolish some frowns.

William Johnstone (10)
Hartford Manor Primary School and Nursery, Hartford

One Day I Went To School And Went In A Pool

One day I went to school and went in a pool
It was cool
Cool and smooth
My friend Quinn and me got out of the pool
And went into school.

Dottie Briscall (7)
Hartford Manor Primary School and Nursery, Hartford

Unicorn

I close my eyes and in my dreams
A unicorn flies
Under sparkly skies
Its horn so bright
Guides dreams through the night.

Eleanor Kettle (6)
Hartford Manor Primary School and Nursery, Hartford

Dream House

D airy Milk castles with milk doors,
R ainbow rain that pops when touched,
E nter the candy wonderland to eat everything,
A fter you enter the house it turns into a robot,
M ilk drops from the house's arms and legs.

H ouse-made with chocolate and Jolly Ranchers,
O pen the door to the smell of candy,
U nder the stairs of marshmallows,
S lides into the room of Sour Patch,
E normous posts of gummy bears.

Abel Jackson (8)
Oakwood Primary School, Easter House

Wintertime

W inter is as cold as snow
I n the winter, the snowball fights go *boom!*
N othing stops us from having fun
T he top of the snowman's head has a black hat
E nter the biggest snow globe ever!
R eally wrap up cosy and warm
T eamwork makes a big snowman
I nto winter we go
M arshmallows on the top of warm hot chocolates
E verybody loves dreaming of winter!

Katerina Spanellis (8)
Oakwood Primary School, Easter House

My Dream House

My dreamhouse has pink and blue wallpaper with rainbow sprinkles outside
There is an ice cream dog and his house is made of peanut butter
His friend breaks his toy but he is fine about it
Then a bully comes and jumps on his house
Smash!
He is furious
The bully laughs at the ice cream dog
The ice cream dog growls at the bully so he runs away.

Ailidh Low (8)
Oakwood Primary School, Easter House

Dream Castle

Once upon a dream,
I built a dream castle.
It was as big as a giraffe.
My giant castle had a lot of land
Made with bourbons, pie, metal fences,
Brick, cake and ice cream.
It goes *boom* and *bang*
When it's under attack.
My guards protect my castle.

George McQuade (8)
Oakwood Primary School, Easter House

Dreams

D reams come true in your mind like you're thinking,
R est in the feeling of dreaming,
E xciting dreams come to you,
A t night, dreams come to everyone,
M ind is your dreams,
S illy dreams are very funny.

Edie-Beau Bunton (8)
Oakwood Primary School, Easter House

Once Upon A Dream

Space is as quiet as a mouse,
It is very dark and creepy,
When you land you can hear normal voices,
People all standing waiting,
I walk out of the spaceship,
All the people cheer.

Lewis McNally (9)
Oakwood Primary School, Easter House

The Steeple Chase

As I got on my horse,
Getting ready for the course.
I had a strange feeling,
As if I was bleeding.
It was my horse,
Had someone covered him in sauce?
But no matter how many times I wanted to get off,
I was forced to stay on.
I walked to the chariot,
Maybe she's here, Auntie Harriet?
I saw the flagmen walk up the stairs,
Not going to lie; they looked like chunky bears.
"Three, two..." went the timekeeper,
"Go!"

I raced my heart out,
We were in front like a pig's snout.
Hurdle number one,
Hurdle number two,
We were leaping over the hurdle,
Until the last one...

We were galloping on,
But in the air, he was done.
We fell to the ground,
I jumped to my feet with a bound.
I raced to my horse,
Whining on the floor of the course.
He couldn't move his neck.
He was gone.
Tears poured out of my eyes,
Not ready for our goodbyes.

I lay next to him for comfort.
"Enid!" said Mum.
It was all just a dream,
And my horse was alive!
So, I got ready to thrive.

Rebecca Foster (10)
Pennthorpe School, Rudgwick

The Forest At Sunset

I looked at the sunset,
It gave me most perfect mindset,
I walked into the forest,
I thought about naming a bear Boris.

In the distance I could see,
A white object, was it a bunny?
It was running towards me rapidly,
It then started chasing a bee.

I sat down on a log,
And started reading a blog.
Then I set up my tent,
I was very afraid that it could've bent.

The animals started to surround me,
Luckily there wasn't a bee,
There were loads of birds,
They were obviously in herds.

Tweet! Tweet! Tweet!
The birds were now on my feet.
It was now time for bed
It was time to rest my head,
For the school day ahead.

Maisie Watkins (10)
Pennthorpe School, Rudgwick

My Friend Cloudy

My friend Cloudy,
Is swifter than an Audi,
He whisps through the sky,
Feeling like the luckiest guy,
He sometimes feels quite alone,
Being the only cloud to be known.

He always looks down at children,
All with their little kittens,
Until one day I find Cloudy,
And I go up to him and say, "Howdy!"
We play together every day,
"I love Cloudy!" I always say.

Until, all of a sudden, I see black,
And I wake up by giving myself a whack,
Then I become sad because Cloudy's gone,
And I realise that, out of all my past dreams, that one shone.

So, whenever you see a cloud,
If you dismiss it, you'll forget it from then on.

James Pinder (10)
Pennthorpe School, Rudgwick

Sunset Forest

As the sun fell it left an ombre of colours light
Suddenly, I'm whisked into the forest at night
Orange, red, blue, yellow and pink
I wanted to close my eyes, just for a wink!

As I looked at the blue sapphire river
The temperature dropped and made me shiver
The river reflected the stars and the moon
And that's when I knew that I would be home soon
The river ran into a lake filled with stars
It was almost like a race of cars

As I walked into the forest late at night
I knew nothing there would give me a fright
Can you feel the magical air?
Can you see the fox with orange hair?
All the animals snug in bed
And there is nothing I would dread!

Lara Hinchey (11)
Pennthorpe School, Rudgwick

The Magic Of A Dream

The magic of a dream,
Makes things seem so real,
It makes even happiness bow down to kneel,
It is like the end of the world when you're forced to wake up,
But in the end, you must be grown up,
And get out of bed but let's not talk about that,
For it is like the end of a chat,
For the magic of a dream is so vitally important,
It is like you are in your own world that the happiness is absorbent.

The magic of a dream,
Is like a happiness stream,
That flows down your body,
It is like drinking a hot toddy,
The dream's power is so mighty,
It floats around you so lightly,
The magic of a dream,
Oh, the magic of a dream.

William Pinder (10)
Pennthorpe School, Rudgwick

What's Under The Bed

Arghh, nightmares, nightmares, everywhere,
Over here and over there,
Clowns, spiders, what's under the bed?
For a second I thought I was dead.
Werewolves with their hands,
And bears with their growls,
Aliens landing in the yard,
Wait, what's that, it's just a guard.
Now I'm definitely dead, and full of extra dread,
And I still haven't checked under the bed,
Arghh, I checked under the bed, it's a creepy doll from the undead,
I'm petrified, it was its eyes, they're roaring red, just like the bed,
Hold on, does it talk? If so, I'm getting out of bed.
Nightmares!

Oliver Bristow (11)
Pennthorpe School, Rudgwick

The Waterfall

The water was clear and blue,
It fell gently from the waterfall.

The flowers all around it,
They lit up my eyes with happiness and joy.

I couldn't work out what it was,
Maybe it was a god crying,
Or maybe the end of the world?

"Don't think like that," I said,
Because the world is fine,
That's what I thought
Until I died.

Before I entered, I heard a sound,
"Tweet."
I was curious.

I wondered for a bit, but then it went black.
I woke up in my bed.

I was sad,
But every dream has to come to an end.

Olivia Church (11)
Pennthorpe School, Rudgwick

The Last Jump

I get into bed and dream,
And put on my Sol de Janeiro.
With a smile on my face,
I dream about a race.
With me and my horse,
Completing a badminton course.
We're at the starting line,
Awaiting a sign.
For the signal to go,
With me and my horse laying low.
Three,
Two,
One,
Go!
And we're off,
We're at the first jump,
Where two riders fall and make a clump.
Then we are at the last leg,
"Can we win?" I beg.
We jump the last jump, tension suddenly rises,
We have won, we get first place prizes.

Aurelie Perkes (11)
Pennthorpe School, Rudgwick

Golden Hour

A brief moment of darkness was all you knew
Before Heaven's Gate came into view

It felt like a dagger in the back
To find out you would no longer be back

As I look up to an angel with wings like arms
And a beautiful halo shining bright gold around her head
She slowly comes towards me
And tells me to go through the gate
To find my mate waiting for me
As we sit there drinking our tea
I suddenly feel a tug on my arm

I awake to my mum telling me to get ready for school!

Zara Watson (11)
Pennthorpe School, Rudgwick

The First Flyer

They are everywhere,
With fancy uniforms,
Big bows and thin shoes,
They do tumbling in them,
And everything else.
When it is stunts, they are nervous,
The first flyer came up in the air,
With big pom poms.
She did her stunts and cradled her down.
Then they couldn't get it the night before,
They were so scared but they did it.
They sat down all together, and
They came first place on the
First competition and the first flyer.

Summer Faulding (10)
Pennthorpe School, Rudgwick

A Dream That Made Me Scream

My night was a fright,
It made me jump
And my head had a bump.
When I walked in the room
There was a boom.

Creak went the floor
As I heard a big roar.
Where am I?
In the devil sky.

Someone needs to help me,
Before I start to scream.
A small light appeared,
Blood up the wall smeared.

Suddenly I scream,
Somebody gave me an ice cream.
Instead of going to hell,
I wake up at the bell.

Anaya Thakkar (10)
Pennthorpe School, Rudgwick

Ted My Friend

I woke up from my bed,
To see my friend Ted,
He was kind and nice,
Gave people their chance twice,
He was my friend,
My friend, Ted.

He may be small,
But gave his all,
It felt unreal,
His house was teal!
He was my friend,
My friend, Ted.

I heard a faint "Bye"
As if I would die,
But it was Ted,
I had to wake from bed,
I'll see him tomorrow,
My friend, Ted.

Arthur Mitchell
Pennthorpe School, Rudgwick

Circus

With a big crowd,
They are clowning around,
It was like a playground.

The tightrope walkers
Were simply street walkers.
They were pretty strong,
It looked really wrong.

The tigers pounce,
The seals bounce,
Husbands and wives
Watch the toffs arrive.

The people were noddy,
And they were having lots of toddy,
They looked really boggy,
Because the clowns made them soppy.

A J Morton
Pennthorpe School, Rudgwick

The Dwellers

They stalk you in the night,
Staying out of sight,
One creeps around toying with you,
The other sneaks in, look out for him too.

If they get to you,
It's already over,
Think what they'll do,
You thought you were helping, by being a prover,
The terror is endless.

Callum Cambell-Yaxley (10)
Pennthorpe School, Rudgwick

Sea Monsters

S uddenly, I heard a sound
E ventually, I knew it was the ground
A s the world began to shake

M ost of the gods were already awake
O ceans, streams and lakes flooded far and wide
N ow something was rising out by my side
"S ea monsters!" I cried! My worst nightmare
T reetops crunched as sea monsters munched
E ating people who cried too much
R ight that second, I was being picked up by a sea monster
S ea monsters! Suddenly, I opened my eyes to find myself in my bed, so nice...

Isabel Starkie Refoios Camejo (9)
St Alban's Catholic Primary School, West Molesey

Countless Dreams

When I'm tired, I go to bed
Dreamy, I rest my head
I transfer into a different world
Each one I hang on every word
But the dream I had tonight was different
It left me feeling quite innocent
First, it began with an Olympic dream
I was the best and on the A team
Then, I moved to a fashion model
Who walked but did not even wobble
My favourite dream came next
One where I was on a quest
But it was no ordinary quest
I had superpowers unlike the rest
I could fly with the moon and stars
Or even decide to take a quick stop on Mars
Whatever I wanted came to life
If I wanted, I could appear with five eyes
But, suddenly, when everything had been embraced
A nightmare slowly took place
I was lost in the woods
With no trace back

And only in clothes and a bright red hat
Putting an end to my countless dreams.

Olivia Shitta (11)
St Alban's Catholic Primary School, West Molesey

The Super Trooper Daze In The Magnificent, Wonderful, Bright Colours!

There was a clown
Bent down
Like a human that fights.
The mess
Adventure, stress
Was like a mistake, misunderstanding.
The horrible villain carefully survived
The extremely cocky villain unexpectedly stopped time
And left everyone surprised.
The evil wizard changed the hungry dinosaurs into clean frogs.
It was crazy
When King Dragon always made the monster the superheroes!
Many people tried to fight
But no one has ever defeated King Dragon at all.
One superhero can
It's called Invisible
But when King Invisible was here

The Super Trooper fought
But Invisible almost failed
Then, King Dangerous died
Because you need to touch the crown or
Crack or *slice!*

Aleksy Stevens (9)
St Alban's Catholic Primary School, West Molesey

Once Upon A Dream

Once upon a dream, I was in a dark night.
Sitting on a tree, it was dark and silent.
I looked around and I saw nothing,
Until I saw rainbow colours coming near me
I looked around
And found
A rainbow fox.
It had a fiery tail.
I touched my heart and I felt coldness
And loneliness
In my heart.
I felt like the world belonged to only me and the fox.
It curled up in my lap and bent its head.
We walked along a dark part and suddenly heard a voice, it said,
"Come to me."
Then, I started running, I ran as fast as my legs could carry me.
I started getting tired and I was slowed down
This creature was getting closer and I was scared.
I saw its shadow and I looked to my left
And saw a small boat and I ran to it.
I jumped in quietly and started rowing.

I rowed as fast as I could but this creature could swim
So it followed me.
I looked for the fox
I could not find it anywhere
As I was getting tired I wondered where the creature went.
I looked around
Saw a small island
And rowed to it.
As I got there, I was grabbed by something huge
I screamed
I woke up
And saw that I was safe in my bed.

David Aneke (12)
St Mary's Catholic Primary School, Madeley

The Dreadful Alarm

When I close my eyes and sleep,
A whole new world is at my feet,
There are tall strong mountains and rivers,
And ice-cold sea that gives me the shivers.
There are plants that reach the top of the skies,
Their colours dazzle my eyes,
But I'm not alone in this place,
There's a creature with a cute and furry face.
I think he wants to be my friend.
But what about when this dream comes to an end?
The flowers and trees will all begin to go away,
Now I wish I could stay,
I shut my eyes, and I hope,
They open, I see a rope,
I start to climb,
But then, I realise, there's no time,
A loud ringing fills my ears,
It's because it's 7am, now I'm in tears.

Cerys Thomas (10)
St Mary's Catholic Primary School, Madeley

Phobias

Phobias are everywhere, I've got them all,
When I'm in a closed-in space I feel so small,
The fear of big objects, they're going to tumble around me,
The fear of being stalked, every move I make you see.
Spiders crawling on my skin, I've got trembling knees,
I feel so cold, do I have frostbite? Will I freeze?
Did I just see myself over there? I'm so confused and I am scared, are we clones?
I'm in a mirror, but everything is so weird.
My reflection is exact, is it bad? So many unknowns.
Now for the rarest phobia of them all,
It's so weird, but true - hang on, arghhh! I've got peanut butter stuck to the top of my mouth!
I mean, what's that all about?

Annabeth Irvine (10)
St Mary's Catholic Primary School, Madeley

The Unexpected Dream

I really love to dream,
As impossible as it might seem,
I close my eyes and then poof!
I'm in another land: I say oof
I land roughly on the ground,
And then I get up and look around,

Someone asks me, "Don't you know?
There's a dragon hiding in the snow,
Look out for his enormous claws,
And also his almighty jaws!"
I knew that to make an escape,
(Before the dragon began to wake),
To the castle across the lake,
I knew it would be harder than baking a cake,

Magically, a pirate appears,
With some almighty spears,
"Do you need help, young lad?
From your face, you look sad,"
"Mr Swashbuckle, please help me,
I absolutely need to flee."
To the castle across the lake,
If you help me, something for you I will bake,"

The pirate agrees, he says, "Okay my lad,
I know that the dragon could be bad,"

We jumped into his pirate ship,
We travelled at a fast clip,
Across the lake we set sail,
I hoped we were not as slow as a snail.
Travelling across the blue lagoon,
I saw some sharks by the light of the moon,
I told the pirate that sharks scare me,
Then I said, "Come and see."
With his spear, the pirate took aim
With my own, I did the same

We threw them at the sharks
Yes! The spears hit their marks,
We got to the castle safe and sound,
We found something leading underground,
We're safe! I wake up, full of relief,
This dream had been beyond belief,
I hope I never have a dream like that ever again.

Jonas Rothwell (8)
St Paul's CE Junior School, Wokingham

My Supreme Superpowers

In the depths of my sleep, a vision takes flight,
A dream dazzling with majestic might,
Where ordinary folks wield powers untold,
Beneath skies bathed in radiant gold,

I soar through the night on wings of desire,
My body transforming, flames flickering higher,
A phoenix reborn, with flames as my crown,
A symbol of strength never to be taken down,

With powers to heal and mend broken hearts,
No longer shackled by human parts,
I touch the wounded, their pain I'll erase,
A healer of souls embracing every phase,

Invisible threads of connection arise,
I see through minds, discern hidden guise,
Telepathic whispers engage in the night,
Unveiling secrets, beyond mere human sight,

With arms outstretched, my touch sparks with might,
An electric surge, illuminating the night,
Harnessing thunder, forging lightening's wrath,
In a symphony of storms, blazing a righteous path,

Leaping through time, with the speed of thought,
Witnessing history, as battles are fought,
I reunite with destiny, shaping a new age,
Championing justice, turning the darkest page,

But as the dream unfolds, a truth starts to gleam,
Superpowers flaunted, aren't quite what they seem,
For true strength lies not in abilities rare,
But in the courage to love, the willingness to care,

So dream on, dear friend, of superpowers divine,
But remember, within you, a hero will shine,
For the power to make a difference and ignite,
Lives within your heart both day and night!

Anvi Mishra (10)
St Paul's CE Junior School, Wokingham

Once Upon A Dream

Last night, I fell asleep late, I
Dreamt about a butterfly,
It didn't start off great,
At first, it made me sigh,
The beautiful blue butterfly was hungry,
But there was no flower to sit,
No pollen to suck, no food to eat,
And nowhere for the butterfly to live,
Sad and furious, nowhere to be safe,
Wondering if it will ever have a place to stay,
How much further, how much further? It has been searching for days,
Will it at least get some food?
It's been starving for days,
There's a bunch of flowers, maybe there's
Some food for it to eat and a home for it to stay in,
It's almost there, just got to flap a bit more,
A home for it at last, but no food for it to eat,

What is happening outside?
"Wow, wow, all the food,
Thank you very much
I've been starving for weeks."
"You can come in if you want.

We can have a small party
We can use all this food,"
I woke up happily and went and
Told my parents what an amazing dream I had.

Akshara Uppuluri (8)
St Paul's CE Junior School, Wokingham

Oh My, I Am A Spy!

This could be my last assignment,
As I close my eyes
And I see the ominous world ahead of me.

A world with laser-shooting hot dogs,
And a skateboard that flies,
Bubblegum that cracks through locks,
The bad guys say bye-byes.

This time, I'm in a cave,
As dark as can be,
There's water all around and,
Cold, sinking into me.

But, I've defeated those who chose
To use their fists instead of voices,
And so many other terrible choices.
I've stopped them from dropping litter,
And making us breathe smoke,
That just makes us choke,
Or using unkind words.
No one's burning any trees,
Or killing any birds.

Now I've told you it was me,
And my cover's blown,
I hope I'm not alone.
That when I'm fully grown,
This isn't a dream,
It's just humanity.

Tomorrow, when I close my eyes,
You might join me in my quest,
To be a good guy -
They're the best.

Gene Coleman (8)
St Paul's CE Junior School, Wokingham

The Nightmare

The dream came as quick as a flash,
Without a splash or even a crash,
Clowns and monkeys grinning wide,
Flew by as I rode my dreamy ride.

Finally, I arrived where I was meant to be,
An abandoned scrapyard next to an eerie quay,
It was quiet, too quiet, as quiet as a mouse,
There wasn't a single person in sight, let alone a house.

A low whistle rang through the air,
And I turned around to see who was there,
But all I saw was a street so bare,
That the silence vibrated everywhere.

A chuckle then graced my ears,
A sound that awakened my deepest fears,
But still, still, there was nothing there,
Only empty, empty air.

A gentle breeze brushed my cheek,
And finally, I saw who I was destined to meet,
A clown who grinned, smiling wide,
Wearing a costume and dyed, blue-eyed.

Then, suddenly, I woke up and nobody was there,
And I realised it had just been a nightmare.

Ethan Ang (11)
St Paul's CE Junior School, Wokingham

The Dragon Disaster

As Hanna opened her eyes,
She saw the beautiful trees of a forest,
She sat up with great surprise,
The forest surroundings were black as night,
Which gave Hanna quite a fright,
Suddenly she was running towards a bright light,
Away from the dark, away from the night,
Before she could get to the light, a wolf crossed her way,
How many battles it had seen, she could not say,
It lunged at her from the dark,
And gave the most ferocious bark,
She had to run quite fast,
The wolf was getting weary at last,
The flaming trees grew bigger,
As a dragon blew with vigour,
She ran to it,
As the fires got lit,
The dragon flicked its tail,
She grabbed onto the cliff with a wail,
Was she close to the ground, it was hard to tell,
Her hand slipped and she fell...

Zoe Tomlinson (10)
St Paul's CE Junior School, Wokingham

A Distant Valley

A distant valley hidden far away, beyond a human's reach.
D ragons fly, soaring into the jet-black sky.
V ictorious mountains huddle close together, surrounding the secret valley.
E lves dwell around whilst admiring the gently sprinkled stars.
N estled griffins doze away, hidden from the glinting planets,
T riumphant trees stay in their spot whilst I relax, feeling quite laid-back.
U nicorns shimmer up high in the sky whilst relaxing clouds pass me by. I settle down feeling as pleased as punch.
R ainbows shine whilst glinting moonlight dances around, I feel as jolly as an elf with a motorcycle.
E bullient, early flowers bloom, creating a strong, soothing aroma, forming a tranquil, peaceful feeling throughout my body.

Laura Hicklin (10)
St Paul's CE Junior School, Wokingham

Giants!

My eyes begin to open,
As I wonder where I am,
My thoughts so deep, it feels like they're spoken,
Where am I? I wondered, am I with Peter Pan in Neverland?
When I looked up, my jaw dropped,
As what I saw was strange,
Houses as big as skyscrapers,
Buildings filled with chefs and dressmakers,
Cars so big they wobbled,
Suddenly, the ground began to shake,
And people started screaming, "The giants, the giants, the giants are awake!"
What's this I should be believing?
But then, I heard a booming voice,
Giants, I thought with dread
Had I made the wrong choice?
I stayed, but I should have fled,
Heart beating fast, I woke up safe in bed,
It was just a dream, all that was in my head!

Kathryn McDonough (10)
St Paul's CE Junior School, Wokingham

Once Upon A Dream

Dreams, dreams,
Are more than they seem,
Good and bad,
Happy and sad,
One night, I was in bed,
Awkward images filled my head,
In the blink of an eye,
I saw the unfriendly sky,
A grey cloud darted towards me,
Striking lightning, everyone could see,
This was when the danger started,
It was the moment the world parted,
There was an issue,
I needed a tissue,
The world felt upside down,
Smiles had turned into frowns,
What was wrong? I had to think,
The floor was as slippery as an ice rink!
"Beware," said the news screen,
"A sneaky ghost has been seen!"
Then, I woke up in the middle of the night,
And said to myself, "Oh, what a fright!"

Aanya Sandeep (9)
St Paul's CE Junior School, Wokingham

Night Shivers

One stormy night,
Something didn't feel quite right,
It gave me a fright.

A set of yellow, beady eyes stared,
Terrorising my soul,
They tore out my bleeding heart and left a gaping hole.

I trembled as I said, "Who's there?"
I know they were hiding,
It was tremendously frightening.

A monstrous figure appeared,
How on earth did he get here?
I was overtaken by indescribable fear.

A bone-crushing look made my skin shiver,
He wore a cloak, towering and sinister,
His face emaciated and covered in blisters.

I fell into darkness,
Awake, awake, awake.

I was so relieved,
It was only a dream.

Georgia Stuart (10)
St Paul's CE Junior School, Wokingham

Skate Penguin

Once I looked out my window,
To hear, to see,
A little black penguin squawking at me,
I had not completed my homework,
I was not done,
But this was my opportunity to have some real fun,
I opened the door and dashed outside,
Only to find something that caused great disappointment inside,
The penguin was gone,
He had vanished without a trace,
Had I imagined his delightful, beaky face?
When suddenly, from the garage arose such a din,
And a black and white flippered form came out from within,
The penguin,
And it appeared he had stolen my top hat and skateboard,
And was wearing a look as if to say,
"I'm that guy, I'm the lord."

Joel Robertson (10)
St Paul's CE Junior School, Wokingham

The Inner Journey

My eyes drifted into darkness,
As I looked at my surroundings,
I was petrified, but curious,
And my heart was pounding.

In the blink of an eye, I was flying,
And the ground was disappearing,
As intriguing as it was,
This was what I'd been fearing.

As I looked below my feet,
Things were gradually getting smaller,
Looking up at the sky,
It was as if I was getting taller.

Suddenly, I was falling,
And soaring through the sky,
I landed with a bash!
And let out a weakening cry.

Seconds later, I woke up
Safe and sound
And that's when I heard a noise
Which made me turn around...

Katerina Hopkins (10)
St Paul's CE Junior School, Wokingham

The Phenomenal Pets!

P art of me was trembling with fear,
H earing a horrifying sound, which was near.
E ither way, I did not know what it could be,
N or did I want to see.
O ak trees rustled in the distance.
M eanwhile, my body froze in an instant.
E erie shadows appeared.
N ow, I bravely peered.
A t last, I could see a harmless wolf and cockerel.
L astly, I felt at ease.

P recisely at that moment, I realised where I was.
E xcitedly, I got up to find myself covered in fluff.
T iny puppies and kittens that I wanted to hug,
S itting on my lap and then I woke up.

Elissa Feist Guerrero (9)
St Paul's CE Junior School, Wokingham

When Fairy Dust Falls!

When fairy dust falls on my feet,
A magical world appears around me.
Then my dogs come barking for treats,
Dozens of bones fall around me,
Then they howl and say goodbye.
I start to get hungry, I start to crave sweets,
But are there any left for me?
Millions, billions, maybe even trillions went into my mouth.
I started smiling, skipping along,
But what's that soaring up high?
A red and white air balloon!
Wow! What a sight!
I start running, racing along.
I sing a song as I go up and up into the horizon.
I close my eyes, and open them and see
I am in my room.
Wow, what a dream!

Millie Simms (10)
St Paul's CE Junior School, Wokingham

Unicorn Dreams

U nderneath the beautiful sparkly starlit sky,
N ight-time comes,
I have never seen a sky like this before!
C louds shimmering and stuttering, dancing around the sky,
O h! I suddenly realise I must be dreaming!
R acing across the sky and onto my clean roof is an eye-catching unicorn,
N ever will I forget this happened.

D reams always can come true,
R arely unicorns show up on your roof,
E agerly, I run to my parents to tell them,
A nd annoyingly it had vanished,
M aybe it will come back?
S o I will keep dreaming.

Freya Moore (10)
St Paul's CE Junior School, Wokingham

The Animal Parade

Parading animals running down my street,
Some tall, some short, some messy, some neat.
An elephant prancing down the road,
A monkey on its shoulders,
A ribbon seal flapping around,
Carrying heavy boulders.
The parrots fly overhead, squawking with delight,
The foxes prowl silently, hidden in the night.
The otter holds the horse's reign,
As the dolphins start to splash again.
A python slithers around the pipe,
Whilst the pigeons preen and wipe.
I scream as a giraffe head pops up,
And I notice a wolf carrying its pup.
The gazelles gallop to and fro,
Whilst cows moo and mow.

Evelyn Clements (10)
St Paul's CE Junior School, Wokingham

Starlight

Starlight shines bright,
First star I saw that night.
I gazed upon the glorious light,
A majestic universe full of planets and comets,
Wow, what a magnificent sight.
Hopping onto my magical ride,
What awaited was an awesome surprise.
The mysterious wizard,
Old and wise,
Cast a spell by my side.
He waved his wand,
Powerful and strong,
Zip and zap,
A ping and a pong.
Suddenly, my star darted across the colourless sky,
I was so excited, I didn't know why.
Was this real?
What was going on in my head?
My alarm was booming,
I woke up in my snuggly bed.

Oliver Radcliffe (9)
St Paul's CE Junior School, Wokingham

Nightmare Forest

Nothing is as it seems,
When I am in my dreams,
The moon is shining so bright,
With all the darkness it gives me such a fright.
As time goes by, it feels like someone is following me,
What could it be, a he or a she?
The owls are noisy and the foxes are cunning,
I'm so scared I can't stop running.
It's dark and I'm so lonely, is anyone there?
Please be a friendly face and not a big, scary bear.
I am so cold, and it won't stop raining,
I promise to go to bed early tomorrow and you won't hear me complaining.
Nothing is as it seems,
When I am in my dreams.

Darcie Withers (8)
St Paul's CE Junior School, Wokingham

Space Dreams

Every night I fall asleep
Each dream I explore
I always look at the floor
But tonight...
My dream gave me a fright
I woke up in space to find I had an alien on my case
"Hello, I'm Mr Bloopbleep," he said to me
"Oh, Mr Bloopbleep, I need to pee"
"I've travelled so far, won't you help me?"
"Come this way
I'll take you to a place
Where you can take your time
And maybe be a friend of mine."
Suddenly, I woke up in bed
To find I had lost my friend
Tonight I'll dream
And hope to see Mr Bloopbleep again...

Lauren Glover (9)
St Paul's CE Junior School, Wokingham

Imagination Unleashes

Every night in my dreams,
Fairies fly, and writers write.
Days and nights passing by
As dancers dance and teachers teach.

Unicorns galloping day by day
Whilst they graze as they may,
Wizards' spells end in laughter,
Wonder Girl saves the town.

Dragons ice-skating on the moonlit sky,
Divers dive all the way down,
As pirates sail their ghostly ship.

Gymnasts twirl and flip,
Kings and queens eating beans,
Cinderella always finds
Her prince eating mince.

Flowers in the sun always bloom,
I don't want to wake up soon.

Ellie Wong (9)
St Paul's CE Junior School, Wokingham

Once Upon A Dream

When I go to sleep at night,
I never have a fright,
Dreaming of a magical world,
Full of trees and bees,
My fairy friends dance and play,
And all night long I want to stay,
The scary dragons breathe their fire,
But all my fairy friends just fly higher,
Zipping through the clouds above,
I suddenly spot a beautiful dove,
We follow it to a clear blue lake,
And land in a meadow to take a break,
Here we love to pick the flowers,
And never keep track of the hours,
Soon, it's time to wake for the day,
But I don't mind, I'll be back to play.

Rosie Harrison (9)
St Paul's CE Junior School, Wokingham

Footballer

F ootsteps away from the field, ready for kick-off.
O ne by one, we stepped up to the pitch.
O verexcited, I heard the referee blow the whistle to start the match.
T he fans started booing and throwing a metal water bottle,
B ecause I scored a marvellous goal.
A fter the referee's decision, the match was abandoned.
L ugubriously, some of my teammates and I got hurt.
L eaving the pitch very unhappily.
E leventy of people fumbling about what happened.
R apidly, I woke up and found that I was safe in bed!

Elvis Poon (9)
St Paul's CE Junior School, Wokingham

Shooting Stars

I can't believe it
I'm flying through outer space
Faster than any meteorite
And more graceful than any shooting star
My skin burns like sausages as I pass Venus
Finding it hard to breathe
I've just passed Jupiter's Great Red Spot
My head spins in circles as Uranus makes me dizzy
As freezing cold as an iceberg, I zoom past Neptune
I fly past Saturn, feeling its icy rings
Gasping at Mars' magnificent red colour
Something catches my eye, a comet!
Suddenly, I wake up, I'm in bed
Was it a dream or not?

Anna Griffin (9)
St Paul's CE Junior School, Wokingham

Footballer

F abulous sport loved by numerous children.
O pportunity of chasing our dream for the future.
O utdoor enjoyment, people eager to do.
T eamwork, spirit building up in the games.
B rilliant moments of shooting to the same goal.
A mbitious sport adored by countless children.
L imitless aspiration of kicking the ball toward the goal.
L aborious mission, people working hard to accomplish.
E nergetic spirit, generating a great collaboration.
R emarkable stars of football might be you!

Jayvis Chan (9)
St Paul's CE Junior School, Wokingham

Childhood Dreams

Not so long ago,
but many years, you know,
I dreamt of things I'd like to do.

When one day I was grown,
of places I'd visit,
and things that I'd create,
of all the fun that I would have.

It seemed too long to wait,
every day, I'd laugh and play.
The world was, oh, so grand!
And destiny was mine to choose.

I held it in my hand,
but now I'm here, I'm not sure where.
Life isn't what it seemed.
I think I'll take another look,
and reclaim my childhood dreams.

Ahmad Alsayd (10)
St Paul's CE Junior School, Wokingham

A Mermaid's Dream

A mystical mermaid cracked open the door,
She sneaked out of the palace, ready to explore.

The sun shone through, touching her glistening scales,
Whilst she swam to the songs of colossal whales.

Her curiosity took her up to the surface,
She was searching for something to give her a purpose.

She glanced at the glistening beach, longing to explore,
A whale came along and swept her gently to shore.

And that's when I woke from magical dreams,
And thought to myself, not everything is as it seems...

Giorgia Alessandrini (9)
St Paul's CE Junior School, Wokingham

Every Day In My Dream

Every day in my dream,
I see a team of aliens who scream,
The stars are sparkling so bright,
I have to close my eyes so tight.

When the lake frost,
I found myself lost,
As scared as a rat chased by a cat.

I saw my sister snap,
She made a rocket with a cap,
I used the rocket to explore the planets,
Then I found a magnet,
I got sucked by the magnet, back to Earth,
And I saw an alien's birth,
I realised I was still in my dream,
And I wonder what's the theme for my next dream.

Adrianna Lau (8)
St Paul's CE Junior School, Wokingham

Crazy Dreams

C ompletely out of control,
R acing in a car without any petrol,
A ccelerating into the unknown,
Z igzagging past pandas riding dinos,
Y ou're in your zone, playing it cool.

D aring, dauntless things you do,
R iding in a magician's car! Wahoo!
E scaping from a giant bull,
A dventures are the only thing you do,
M aking your mark wherever you go,
S uch things, things you can only do, when your dreams become as crazy as they can be!

Gautam Singh (11)
St Paul's CE Junior School, Wokingham

The Supers!

Once upon a time,
There was a superhero called Silver,
Flying in the sky,
He was high and totally shy,
Silver lives in Bath and likes his bubble bath,
He found a dog called Golden on his path,
The dog has superpowers,
Golden was able to fly and run fast,
Suddenly, the city's golden dome was missing,
The news was terrifying,
Silver and Golden were ready to work together,
They were excited to save Bath together,
They were passionate about their mission,
Ready for action!

Arya Partthepan (8)
St Paul's CE Junior School, Wokingham

Once Upon A Dream

In my dreams, fairies fly in the sky,
Like bright, shining stars with all their sparkle,
Glancing left and right,
All I see are stars in the night.
You feel you are in a different land,
Dying to explore what happens next.
The words you will hear in your mind,
You'll feel like fairies are cheering for you in the night.

Hoping when you reach out you'll
Feel something unusual,
Flying and twirling, dropping their sparkles,
You'll see their sparkles and be surprised.

Jiya Shah (7)
St Paul's CE Junior School, Wokingham

Seasonal Changes

Warm sunshine is here at last
Cold winter days are now in the past
Spring leaves are colours bright
Joyful to have reached the uplifting light

In a blink, summer is here
Many new trees and flowers appear

The wind blows, the colours change
Red, orange, yellow and brown
Golden shadows cover the ground

I'm running down a hill
Streams singing around
A glimmering sunbeam shone
My ears were awoken by a birdsong
Opening my eyes, a glorious day ahead.

Isabella Guo (10)
St Paul's CE Junior School, Wokingham

Starlight

S tarlight shining to the Earth's core,
T rees covered in multicoloured spores,
A bundant constellations shimmering in the purple night,
R eflections of the moon shining so bright,
L ighting up the sky like twinkling fairies,
I f you think about it, it is pretty scary,
G oing up out of the Earth's atmosphere,
H igh up and above the horizon, they have no fear,
T umbling asteroids at a fast pace, speeding through infinite space.

Jacob Sheppard (9)
St Paul's CE Junior School, Wokingham

A Place Called Nowhere

Climbing into bed,
All cosy and soft.
Resting your head
And nodding off.
Your mind swirls, whirls and curls.
Then suddenly you're there,
In a place called nowhere.
Wizards and wands,
Trolls in ponds.
Castles of brick,
The size of a stick.
Towers with powers,
Swerving and curving,
Clowns in gowns,
Wearing great big frowns.
But, suddenly, the sky turns white,
And in a fright.
You turn to the right...
Nothing.
Not a speck in sight!

David Purle (11)
St Paul's CE Junior School, Wokingham

Nightmare

It is real dark,
I see a slight spark,
I'm in a big house,
Not a place without a mouse,
I stop, the mouse speaks,
I go back, it squeaks!
I turn around,
I hear a pound,
I'm too scared to wake up,
Why a mouse,
Not a pup?
I feel scared,
Since I'm not paired,
I wish someone was there,
To kill the fear everywhere,
I will wake up, I won't stay,
That's when they'll go away
And I'll dream something else another day.

Leilah Abdelrahim (8)
St Paul's CE Junior School, Wokingham

Fairy Catcher

F luttering and muttering all about
A s the day begins
I wonder and wonder
R eally if the catchers are here
Y es! But such an awful sight

C an they reach?
A ll wonder to each other
"T hey won't find us, will they?" others say
C ameras shutter and click, they are here!
H elp, the monstrosity has come
E ach and every one of us hides and runs
R ace your fairy friends for your life.

Dhruvi G Patel (9)
St Paul's CE Junior School, Wokingham

My Wonderland Gone Wrong

When I close my eyes,
I am very surprised,
To see a dwarf staring back at me,
Was this meant to be?
I turn around and see,
A cotton candy tree,
Also, loads of sweets,
Oh! There are some meats,
Like steak and chicken,
Which will make me thicken,
But I don't care,
I'll stay if there is no air,
So I eat, eat, eat,
'Til everything is concrete,
Now I wanna leave,
The sweet world is what I want to retrieve,
Please, please, please?

Isobel Reid (10)
St Paul's CE Junior School, Wokingham

Nightmares

N estled in the shadows, the mind sets a trap.
I nvisible terrors, nightmares snap.
G hastly clowns with grins so wide.
H orrifying spiders, I sat there and cried.
T rapped in a web of dreams untold.
M ysteries everywhere, a tale to behold.
A tale of darkness, where courage wanes.
R evealing fears, in everyone's brains.
E ach superpower flickers and gleams.
S uddenly, I woke up, it was just a dream.

Sofia Hunt (9)
St Paul's CE Junior School, Wokingham

Horrible Nightmares

I wasn't ready for this horrible night,
As the sun rises, there appears light.
I see a beastly creature,
With fire as its main feature.
Suddenly, I realise it's a dragon,
As it burns the wagon,
And rolls it across the land,
On which my feet stand.
It begins to chase me,
I find a key.
Then I see a door,
As the rain begins to pour.
I run to take shelter,
As I see a helper,
Who gets its knife,
Ready to save my life...

Laiba Khalil (10)
St Paul's CE Junior School, Wokingham

Dreams Big Or Small

You know what's extreme,
An amazing dream,
Maybe you could fly,
Really high,
Or you could be a king or queen,
With some great jeans,
Or even a knight,
Who is an absolute delight,
You could also be a fairy with a unicorn,
With a magical horn,
Or maybe a footballer with amazing goals,
Who's madly famous and who has a great soul,
See, if you dream, you can do whatever you want.
Just dream and don't say you can't!

Arin Sahoo (8)
St Paul's CE Junior School, Wokingham

Dragon Race

D ragons in a field prancing with delight,
R ace starts; we were all ready for a fight.
A nd then they were all up in the air,
G etting ready for the dragon flying fair.
O n 1, 2, 3, the race starts!
N ot a fight, just a chase.

R ats! Another dragon flying with pace.
A lmost done now in the leagues.
C ertificate! I won with glee.
E loiese, my mum, my job is now done.

Zoe Shaw (8)
St Paul's CE Junior School, Wokingham

The Dream Recipe

M ake yourself comfy in your bed,
A nd follow these steps, you sleepy heads,
G row heavy to relax your mind,
I magine the world you may find,
C lose your eyes and drift away,

S ettle down while your thoughts start to play,
T hink of an enchanting land,
A ll around you can hear a mystical band,
R ainbow unicorns, fairies on a quest,
S leep away, a well-needed rest.

Mabel Hodson (8)
St Paul's CE Junior School, Wokingham

Breathing Fire

I stretch my wings up to the sky,
I'm soaring up so high.
My claws are sharp,
Good for catching carp.

My breath is fiery and hot,
One gust, and I just can't stop.
I am vicious and angry,
Especially when I get hangry.

Although I don't often sleep,
When I do, I curl up in a heap.
Now it's time to say goodbye,
And control my venomous bite.

For a new day,
Tomorrow maybe?

Adelaide O'Mahoney (10)
St Paul's CE Junior School, Wokingham

Dreaming Acrostic Poem

D elightful nights can lead to a dreadful night of dreams,
R esting cheerfully can go to a very bad dream,
E erie eyes can look at you while you sleep,
A fraid that someone might weep,
M aking frightful noises that might make you cry loudly,
I magining unreal places deeply,
N ightmares might also be a good one, but it can be very bad,
G orgeous dreams will be the best kind of dream.

Hayden Li (9)
St Paul's CE Junior School, Wokingham

Cursed Cats

C oming from inside a portal,
U nlimited light gleams like it's immortal.
R adiation showers on top of me,
S o I decided to go inside and see.
E verywhere surrounding me,
D ark black cats stare with glee.

C amouflaged in the dark surroundings,
A small black cat runs to my founding.
T aunted by it, I run away,
S o it was just a dream, hooray!

Aarna Singh (11)
St Paul's CE Junior School, Wokingham

Just A Dream

A magical world shaped around me,
With singing flowers and dancing trees,
There was even a lime-green bee!
In this place, I felt so free.
I flew above the trees, didn't worry about a thing!
I met pirates, and friended fairies,
But who knew that my alarm was going to ring?
I sat on dinosaurs and flying ponies...
Then I woke up and sat on my bed,
"Oh," I said, "it was all just a dream!"

Shiona Chatterjee (11)
St Paul's CE Junior School, Wokingham

Against All Odds

Today is match day, although anything could happen,
Winning at the Etihad, I could only imagine,
Champions of Europe, kings at home,
Was it time for Little Brentford to knock them off their throne?
Little against large, a mismatch on paper,
Did things go as expected? You'll find out later!
I'll give you a clue, things didn't go to plan,
Manchester City 1, Brentford 2, Ivan Toney was the man!

Noah Brocklehurst-Waite (9)
St Paul's CE Junior School, Wokingham

Magic Land

My dream last night,
Fairies whizzing in groups of light,
Wizards waving their magic canes,
The flying horses shake their manes,
Mermaids swimming whilst singing a song,
Accompanied dolphins for so long.
All that shines is the bright pink sky,
Dancers gliding in the skating rink nearby,
But they don't stay for long, they disappear,
Maybe I'll have to wait 'til next year...

Iris Yan (9)
St Paul's CE Junior School, Wokingham

Friendship

To care for a friend is what I like to do.
Make them feel happy and laugh till we're blue.
Go to the park and play basketball
Or even go to the mall.
Have an ice cream in the summertime.
Grape bubblegum or even lime.
Grow up and cry about life's heartaches.
Get over it, work together, whatever it takes.
I will be with my friends all the way through
Until I'm about 102.

Mithat Kaur (10)
St Paul's CE Junior School, Wokingham

Sparkles And Me

In my dream the kitty land,
Kittens running and playing cars,
Sparkles the kitten flies up high,
Sparkles asked me, "Who am I?"
"I am Skye," I said by
Sparkles born with magical powers,
She turns straw into golden flowers,
Greedy cat robber, loves the gold,
Catnap, Sparkles on the road,
Police come to save her life,
Magical powers take robber's knife.

Skye Chow (7)
St Paul's CE Junior School, Wokingham

Rainforest

R aindrops fall on the mossy floor,
A s monkeys chatter, swing and sway,
I nsects crawl on the sticky sap,
N ew flowers bloom,
F lying parrots squawk like piercing screams,
O ver the dancing trees,
R ipples of water merge to a lake,
E verything is quiet,
S nakes slither green and long,
T rying to wrap around the trees.

Maia Garwood (10)
St Paul's CE Junior School, Wokingham

Singing Clowns

I went to sleep counting sheep,
I looked up and down and then I saw a clown,
I walked down the path,
But I didn't know if the clown
Was only trying to make me laugh.

So I walked back to him and I was wrong,
So he walked towards me singing a creepy song.

Then I woke up with a fright,
It was only a dream,
Then I looked out the window and no
Light was seen.

Jaya-Belle Barkes (8)
St Paul's CE Junior School, Wokingham

Dreams

There I lay in my bed,
Creations swimming in my head,
Bursting with imagination,
Surely a wonderful sensation,
Seeing things that I desire,
Something I may wish to acquire,
Superheroes and fantasy,
Myths of melancholy,
Experiencing a whole new universe,
Amazing creatures,
Unique and diverse,
An excellent thing it may seem,
For that is what you call a dream...

Sujay Venkatesh (8)
St Paul's CE Junior School, Wokingham

Dreamlight

As I climb over rainbow clouds,
I climb up unicorn mounds,
I can run over rainbows happily,
All the unicorns are walking hungrily,
I do cartwheels across the cloudy country,
A unicorn told me bluntly,
Not to go beyond the hills,
For there is a dangerous mill,
I went back to where I landed,
Then fell out of my dream stranded,
My bed all comfy,
Not at all lumpy.

Violet Perry (9)
St Paul's CE Junior School, Wokingham

The Aurora

Oh, Northern Lights,
Oh, so bright!
Your colours fill the night,
With every peer,
My glance comes near,
To thy wonderful sight,
Oh, Northern Lights!
Oh, Northern Lights!
When you dance with me,
I'm filled with glee.
As I meander through the sea,
You're the key to my fantasy.
Oh, Northern Lights!
Oh, Northern Lights!
Set me free!

Natanya Philip (10)
St Paul's CE Junior School, Wokingham

Dreaming

D rifting off to sleep.
R eady to dream.
E xcited to spray a hot dog masterpiece.
A bandoned train stations make a good canvas.
M inding my own business.
I take out my spray can, eager to start.
N ervously looking over my shoulder, not sure I'm supposed to be doing this.
G raffiti helps me to express my feelings.

Nathaniel Watson (10)
St Paul's CE Junior School, Wokingham

Food World

Food World is a place made out of food
It's a new world where everything is made out of food
And whenever you take a bite out of something
It doesn't go
It just stays there
Never goes
But it never stays
It does in mind
Because reality is fake in his world
It doesn't exist
It's all just a dream...

Alfie Nicoll (10)
St Paul's CE Junior School, Wokingham

Candy Land

C andy is everywhere!
A nd there is enough for a whole school to share!
N ever-ending and all around!
D olly mixtures, Haribos, jelly beans!
Y um yum!

L ovely candies fill my mind!
A nd everything swirls!
N ice and cosy in my bed!
D reams are nice in my head!

Holly Haskins (9)
St Paul's CE Junior School, Wokingham

Fairy Magic

In my dream last night,
Fairy flew with colour bright.
There was a lovely star she found,
To put on her fairy wand.
With a twinkle in her eyes,
To make the magic always tries,
Make a wish with her bright wings,
The song with beautiful voice she sings.
Spinning, spinning and spinning,
To make your dreams come true.

Sin Yan Ying (10)
St Paul's CE Junior School, Wokingham

The Morning Rise And The Weekly Drive

I woke up in a fright,
As my cat gave me a bite!
So I rose,
From my daily dive,
And taught my cat,
Not to bite!

While on my weekly drive,
I was going this time,
To get shopping,
While I was hopping,
Singing along to my favourite song,
Thinking of playing ping-pong,
Meeting my dad on the way!

Dennis Eaglesham (9)
St Paul's CE Junior School, Wokingham

We Need To Protect Our World

Ride, ride, ride, your bike,
Plant, plant, plant some trees,
Save, save, save the bees,
Go, go, go for a hike.

We need to reuse,
We need to recycle,
We need to reduce.

Leave, leave, leave your car,
Give, give, give your toys,
To young girls and boys.

Without your car,
You can still go very far.

Oscar Campbell (9)
St Paul's CE Junior School, Wokingham

Once Upon A Black Hole

B izarre objects,
L ying at the centre of galaxies,
A fabric tear in space,
C ollapsed star,
K illing light - there's no escape,

H oles in the cosmos,
O utbursts of celestial X-rays,
L eading to the unknown,
E xploding supernova wakes me from my dream.

Nikòs Cheema (8)
St Paul's CE Junior School, Wokingham

Writing For Hollywood

Toy Story, Moana, I wrote them all,
But in my mind, they're not the same,
Toys come alive, but age and grow,
And life is just one big game.

A young girl on an island paradise,
She listens to the voices from the sea,
Diving in and becoming a beautiful mermaid,
And knows this is where she was always meant to be.

Alice Dimmock (10)
St Paul's CE Junior School, Wokingham

Sleep Tight

When I sleep, I close my eyes,
And think about a nice surprise,
Will it be something good to eat?
Or something to make me tap my feet?
Dancing sloths or singing giraffes,
Something to make me scream and laugh,
When you dream, there are no limits,
The world is your playground,
So with two feet, jump right into it.

Fraiser Warner (10)
St Paul's CE Junior School, Wokingham

Nature Poem

N ew leaves are forming, as far as I can see,
A nd I look up, the trees are bigger than me.
T he birds all sing loudly, the bees buzz happily,
U nderneath the canopy, the horses run freely.
R iding my scooter, I feel I could fly,
E verything is warm, the sun shines high in the sky.

Daisy Rao (10)
St Paul's CE Junior School, Wokingham

Exploration

In my dreams, every night,
I see a bright, shining light,
I walk through it like a deer,
To explore evermore,
I've trekked across the desert,
Under the fiery sun,
I drifted across the sand,
In a jeep, which was grand,
What a lovely time I've had,
Then my alarm went off,
I was so mad.

Arjun Ravi (10)
St Paul's CE Junior School, Wokingham

Football

F amous ball,
O h, become my baller,
O ver my head it goes,
T aking over my mind, it knows,
B all goes flying to the moon,
A n astronaut will come at noon,
L anding on the grubby surface,
L aunching me out of my dream consciousness.

Charlie Peacock (8)
St Paul's CE Junior School, Wokingham

Meet The King

I want to meet the King of Spain,
I go to the airport but there is no plane,
I go to the ferry but the ship sinks,
I go to the station but there is no train to Spain,
Finally, I walk to Spain, under the rain,
And the king rewards me with a ring,
I understand that no pain, no gain.

Muffin Tang (9)
St Paul's CE Junior School, Wokingham

Pokémon Fantasy

P artnering with friends,
O ff to the Alola region.
K nock back obstacles, running through trees.
É nergising my throwing skills.
M oving rapidly.
O ver, up on the green hill, was a Pokémon.
N ow, onto the next...

Theo Dunmow (9)
St Paul's CE Junior School, Wokingham

Dragon

Dragon, dragon, in the sky,
Flies so high it touches the sky.
Red and fierce, breathing fire,
Flying, flying, higher, higher.

Dragon, dragon, in a cave,
He's not scared, he's so brave.
Eyes glisten in the dark,
Lighting the cave with a spark.

Sadie Grinter (10)
St Paul's CE Junior School, Wokingham

My Cats

When I'm asleep, all I hear is
Miaow, miaow, miaow, miaow.
Then, when I wake, I can hear
Purr, miaow, miaow.
My cat is loud and noisy,
She makes me feel happy, calm and relaxed.
Her first purr is what makes me know
She is happy too.

Isaac Gosling Baker (9)
St Paul's CE Junior School, Wokingham

Dreams

D reams are your imagination flying through your mind,
R acing around your head as you sleep
E very single night.
A lthough you might not remember
M uch of what happens,
S leep well, and try to remember tonight.

Bethan Kirkaldy (9)
St Paul's CE Junior School, Wokingham

The Amazing Fairies

Fairies have an amazing land
It is right among the sand
The fairies jump up and down
In the air, on the ground
They each have a pet dog
And that is called hound
In a palace is where it's found
On a cloud that's very round.

Irhaa Gillani (8)
St Paul's CE Junior School, Wokingham

Dragon

D ragons fly in the sky
R aging with fire from a big sigh
A ges ago there used to be lots
G o on down and detangle the knots
O ne day there may have been lots, but probably not now...
N ever say never.

Anjana Senthil Kumar (10)
St Paul's CE Junior School, Wokingham

Dream, Dream, Dream

Dream, dream, dream,
Dreams are like stars,
There are millions of them.
Dreams give us light,
Dreams rely on imagination.
Some dreams could be dark,
Dreams illuminate us,
Dream, dream, dream.

Fraser Rhodes (10)
St Paul's CE Junior School, Wokingham

Dragons

D angerous, sharp teeth
R oars so ferociously
A mazing strong wings
G raceful if helped
O bedient to you
N oble and kind
S tays with you for life.

Fatimah Asad (10)
St Paul's CE Junior School, Wokingham

Winter Weather

The horses walked
Down the street,
There were feet
Covered in sleet.

The winter weather,
Then came a feather,
Cold as it is,
Always be bold.

Ameya Sunil (9)
St Paul's CE Junior School, Wokingham

YOUNG WRITERS INFORMATION

We hope you have enjoyed reading this book – and that you will continue to in the coming years.

If you're a young writer who enjoys reading and creative writing, or the parent of an enthusiastic poet or story writer, do visit our website **www.youngwriters.co.uk**. Here you will find free competitions, workshops and games, as well as recommended reads, a poetry glossary and our blog.

If you would like to order further copies of this book, or any of our other titles, then please give us a call or visit **www.youngwriters.co.uk**.

Young Writers
Remus House
Coltsfoot Drive
Peterborough
PE2 9BF
(01733) 890066
info@youngwriters.co.uk

YoungWritersUK   YoungWritersCW
youngwriterscw   youngwriterscw